The True Story of the
CIVIL WAR

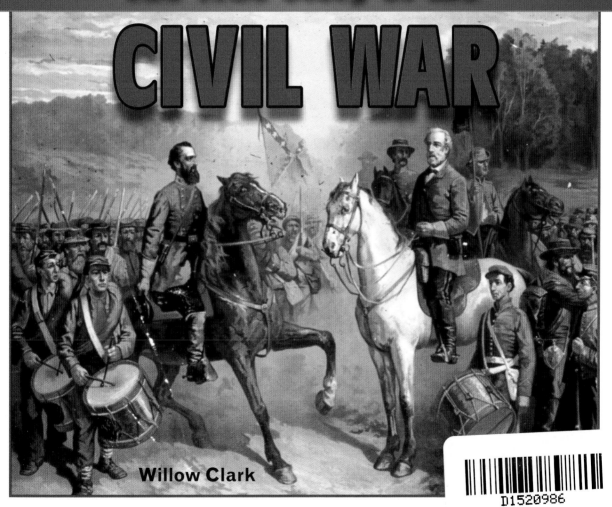

Willow Clark

PowerKiDS press.

New York

Published in 2013 by The Rosen Publishing Group, Inc.
29 East 21st Street, New York, NY 10010

Copyright © 2013 by The Rosen Publishing Group, Inc.

First Edition

Editor: Amelie von Zumbusch
Book Design: Colleen Bialecki

Photo Credits: Cover, pp. 11, 15 MPI/Stringer/Archive Photos/Getty Images; p. 5 Images Etc Ltd/Photographer's Choice RF/Getty Images; p. 7 Jupiter Images/Comstock Images/Getty Images; p. 9 George Eastman House/Archive Photos/Getty Images; p. 13 The Lexington of 1861, pub. by Currier and Ives, c. 1861 (colour litho, American School (19th century)/American Antiquarian Society/Worcester, Massachusetts, USA/The Bridgeman Art Library; p. 17 Photo Researchers/Getty Images; p. 19 Winslow Homer/The Bridgeman Art Library/Getty Images; p. 21 Visions of America/Universal Images Group/Getty Images.

Library of Congress Cataloging-in-Publication Data

Clark, Willow.
 The true story of the Civil War / by Willow Clark. — 1st ed.
    p. cm. — (What really happened?)
 Includes index.
 ISBN 978-1-4488-9693-6 (library binding) — ISBN 978-1-4488-9844-2 (pbk.) —
 ISBN 978-1-4488-9845-9 (6-pack)
 1. United States—History—Civil War, 1861–1865—Juvenile literature. I. Title.
 E468.C66 2013
 973.7—dc23
                                    2012033062

Manufactured in the United States of America

CPSIA Compliance Information: Batch #W13PK4: For Further Information contact Rosen Publishing, New York, New York at 1-800-237-9932

CONTENTS

WHAT WAS THE CIVIL WAR?

A civil war is a war between two or more groups within a country. The American Civil War took place between 1861 and 1865. It was fought between the North and the South. The South was also known as the Confederate States of America. The North was also called the Union.

The Civil War has been called many names over the years, such as the War Between the States. The war cost thousands of lives on both sides. It brought an end to slavery in the United States and brought the North and the South back together as one country.

The United States has thousands of Civil War monuments. This one honors soldiers from Virginia who fought in the Battle of Gettysburg, in Gettysburg, Pennsylvania.

GROWTH AND COMPROMISES

In the 1800s, the South's **economy** relied on African American slaves to grow crops on large **plantations**. These states became known as slave states. States in the North **abolished** slavery in the 1700s and early 1800s. Their economies depended more on factories than on plantation farming. States that outlawed slavery were called free states.

During the nineteenth century, the United States grew quickly. When states joined the country, they were admitted as either free or slave states. Both kinds of states wanted to increase their numbers since that meant there would be more people representing their side in the national government. They argued and made **compromises** about admitting new states.

Many of the Southern plantations that depended on slaves grew cotton. Factory workers in the North and Europe made the cotton into cloth.

FORMING A CONFEDERACY

By the 1850s, the United States was bitterly divided over the spread of slavery. In the 1860 presidential election, the issue came to a breaking point. Republican **candidate** Abraham Lincoln said he wanted to stop the spread of slavery. The other three candidates either supported the spread of slavery or took no stand on the issue.

After Lincoln won the election, South Carolina **seceded**, or broke away from the rest of the United States. Mississippi, Florida, Alabama, Georgia, Louisiana, and Texas soon followed. Together they formed the Confederate States of America. Jefferson Davis was sworn in as its president in 1861.

On February 22, 1861, Lincoln raised a 34-star American flag at Independence Hall in Philadelphia, Pennsylvania. It had one star for each state, including those that had just seceded.

STARTING THE WAR

When the first Southern states seceded, there were still a few federal properties, such as forts, within their territories. One of these was Fort Sumter, which lies off the coast of Charleston, South Carolina. The Confederacy wanted Union troops to leave these properties so that they could take them over. President Lincoln wanted to keep them under Union control and be able to supply them peacefully.

On April 12, 1861, Confederate forces fired on Fort Sumter. After 34 hours of battle, Union troops **surrendered** the fort. This Confederate victory marked the beginning of the Civil War.

Nobody was killed in the Battle of Fort Sumter. However, an accident during the ceremonies at which the fort was turned over to the Confederates killed two people.

SUPPORTING THE WAR

The Southern victory at Fort Sumter convinced Virginia, North Carolina, Arkansas, and Tennessee to secede and join the Confederacy. Not all slave states joined the Confederacy, though. Missouri, Kentucky, Maryland, and Delaware were slave states that stayed on the Union side. They were known as border states.

Not everyone in the South supported the Confederacy, either. In fact, every Confederate state except for South Carolina sent at least one unit of Union soldiers into battle! The people of West Virginia seceded from Virginia and joined the Union in 1863.

Some Northerners supported the war because the Confederates fired first. Many wanted to keep the country together, too.

Some people in border states supported the South. On April 19, 1861, Confederate supporters in Baltimore, Maryland, fought Union soldiers in what is now known as the Baltimore Riot.

WHO FOUGHT IN THE WAR?

At the beginning of the Civil War, both the Union and the Confederacy relied on men to **volunteer** to be soldiers. In 1862, the Confederacy began to **draft** soldiers. In 1863, the Union did, too. The draft meant that men had to sign up for military service and report for duty when they were asked. However, men also could pay money to get out of the draft.

About 15 percent of Confederate soldiers and 6 percent of Union soldiers were draftees. The rest of the soldiers were volunteers or substitutes who had been paid to serve in the place of other men.

Robert E. Lee (center) was a leading Confederate general. Lincoln offered Lee the command of the Union army in April 1861. Lee turned the offer down after Virginia seceded.

AFRICAN AMERICANS

While some people say there were many African American Confederate soldiers, that is incorrect. There were some slaves who went to war with their owners or were forced to do labor for the Confederacy. However, African Americans were banned from serving as Confederate soldiers until the war was nearly over. The few that served after the ban was lifted did not see much action.

African Americans began fighting for the Union partway through the war. In 1863, President Lincoln passed the **Emancipation Proclamation**. It freed slaves in the Confederate states and allowed African Americans to join the Union army.

By the end of the Civil War, more than 186,000 African American soldiers joined the Union army. About half came from the Confederate states.

A SOLDIER'S LIFE

Civil War soldiers wore hot, scratchy uniforms made of heavy wool, even in the summer. Confederate soldiers' uniforms tended to be more worn than those of Union soldiers. The Confederacy had less money and supplies than the Union.

On both sides, more soldiers died from diseases or from **infected** wounds than were killed in battle. About one in four Union soldiers were killed or wounded, and about one in three Confederate soldiers were killed or wounded. By the end of the war, the total number of dead was around 620,000. Of that number, around 360,000 were Union soldiers and 260,000 were Confederate soldiers.

Life was hard for Civil War soldiers. Confederate soldiers struggled to find food. Hard crackers, called hardtack, were the Union soldiers' main food. Both sides had delays in paying soldiers.

ONE NATION ONCE MORE

On April 9, 1865, Confederate General Robert E. Lee surrendered to Union General Ulysses S. Grant, ending the war. Abraham Lincoln was killed just a week later, on April 15. The country began Reconstruction, the process of becoming one nation again. Reconstruction lasted from 1865 until 1877.

Three **amendments** were added to the United States' Constitution during this period. The Thirteenth Amendment outlawed slavery. The Fourteenth Amendment granted citizenship to former slaves. The Fifteenth Amendment gave voting rights to male former slaves. However, many states and cities passed laws, called Jim Crow laws, which limited the rights of African Americans.

Lee surrendered to Grant at the McLean House in Appomattox Court House, Virginia, after the Confederacy lost the Battle of Appomattox Court House.

WHAT REALLY HAPPENED?

The main issue dividing the Union and the Confederacy during the Civil War was slavery. However, war broke out over the right of states to secede. We know how the focus of the war changed from speeches and **documents** written by leaders on each side.

Civil War soldiers fought for many reasons. Some wanted to end slavery, others to preserve it. Some fought because of loyalty to their country or because they were drafted. We know about these soldiers through the letters and diaries they wrote. Studying these speeches, documents, letters, and diaries gives us a richer picture of what really happened in the Civil War.

GLOSSARY

abolished (uh-BAH-lishd) Did away with.

amendments (uh-MEND-ments) Additions or changes to the Constitution.

candidate (KAN-dih-dayt) A person who runs in an election.

compromises (KOM-pruh-myz-ez) Agreements reached by both sides giving up something.

documents (DOK-yoo-ments) Written or printed statements that give official information about something.

draft (DRAFT) To pick people for a special purpose.

economy (ih-KAH-nuh-mee) The way in which a country or a business oversees its goods and services.

Emancipation Proclamation (ih-man-sih-PAY-shun pro-kluh-MAY-shun) A paper, signed by Abraham Lincoln during the Civil War, that freed all slaves held in Southern territory.

infected (in-FEK-ted) Became sick from germs.

plantations (plan-TAY-shunz) Very large farms where crops are grown.

seceded (sih-SEED-ed) Withdrew from a group or a country.

surrendered (suh-REN-derd) Gave up.

volunteer (vah-lun-TEER) To offer oneself for service in the military.

INDEX

WEBSITES

Due to the changing nature of Internet links, PowerKids Press has developed an online list of websites related to the subject of this book. This site is updated regularly.
Please use this link to access the list:
www.powerkidslinks.com/wrh/cwar/